How to Write Your Best Story EVER!

First edition for North America published in 2016
by Barron's Educational Series, Inc.

First published in 2015 by Oxford University Press
Great Clarendon Street, Oxford OX2 6DP

All inquiries should be addressed to:
Barron's Educational Series, Inc.
250 Wireless Boulevard
Hauppauge, NY 11788
www.barronseduc.com

ISBN: 978-1-4380-0909-4

Library of Congress Control No.: 2015960041

Date of Manufacture: April 2016
Manufactured by: Leo Paper Products, Kowloon, Hong Kong

Printed in China

9 8 7 6 5 4 3 2 1

How to Write Your Best Story EVER!

Written by **Christopher Edge**

Illustrated by **Nathan Reed**

BARRON'S

CONTENTS

6
Introduction

8
How to Use This Book

10
Story Sparks

14
Creating Characters

18
Setting the Scene

22
What's the Plot?

26
Storytelling

30
Starting Your Story

34
Action!

38
Making It Real

42
Talk the Talk

46
Creative Vocabulary

50
The End

54
Choosing a Title

56
Is It Finished?

60
How to Write Your Best
ADVENTURE STORY Ever!

64
How to Write Your Best
MYSTERY STORY Ever!

68
How to Write Your Best
SCARY STORY Ever!

72
How to Write Your Best
FUNNY STORY Ever!

76
How to Write Your Best
FANTASY STORY Ever!

80
How to Write Your Best
SCIENCE FICTION STORY Ever!

84
How to Write Your Best
SPY STORY Ever!

88
How to Write Your Best
LOVE STORY Ever!

92
How to Write Your Best
HISTORICAL STORY Ever!

96
How to Write Your Best
DIARY STORY Ever!

100
How to Write Your Best
ANIMAL STORY Ever!

104
How to Write Your Best
SPORTS STORY Ever!

108
How to Write Your Best
SCHOOL STORY Ever!

112
How to Write Your Best
THRILLER STORY Ever!

116
How to Write Your Best
SCRIPT Ever!

120
How to Write Your Best
MASH-UP STORY Ever!

124
Read All About It!

126
Index

INTRODUCTION

So you want to write your best story ever?
Whether it's an action-packed adventure filled with
rogue spies and super-villains, a heart-breaking
romance about two lovesick robots, or a
laugh-out-loud doodle diary about the
biggest geek in school, you'll find
everything you need in this book.

KAZOOOOOM!

There are hints and tips to help you create incredible characters and amazing settings, and think up eye-poppingly exciting plots. Take a spin in the word webs to discover weird and wonderful words that will put the **WOW** into your story, and find inspiration with lines from fantastic fiction and awesome advice from a children's author.

The best writers might know all the rules about writing, but they aren't afraid to break them too. You don't even have to worry about any boring grammar stuff as red alerts will help you to spot any mistakes you might make and make sure your story is the best it can be.

All you need to add is your imagination. So what are you waiting for? Turn the page and start writing your best story ever!

Christopher Edge

HOW TO USE THIS BOOK

This is a book of two halves —both filled with **fantastic ideas** and **advice**!

In the **first half** of the book, you'll find everything you need to know about writing a story from start to finish —from finding inspiration and ideas to checking the final product, and EVERYTHING ELSE in between!

The **second half** of the book gives you hints and tips about how to write different types of story from **adventures** and **mysteries** to **comic book scripts** and **mash-ups**, too. You can read the book from cover to cover or jump from page to page to find the advice you need.

WORD WEBS

Use the word webs to help you find the right words for your story—from action verbs to vocabulary that is out of this world. If you can't find the word you're looking for, take a peek in a dictionary or thesaurus—use the word web as a starting point to spin your own creative vocabulary. The walking thesaurus and dictionary characters will be making appearances throughout this book!

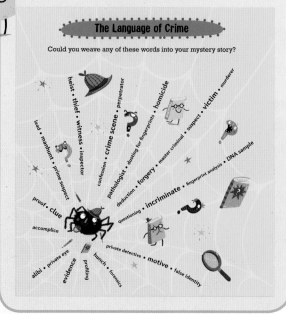

The Language of Crime

Could you weave any of these words into your mystery story?

heist • thief • witness • inspector
lead • manhunt • prime suspect
confession • crime scene • perpetrator
pathologist • dusting for fingerprints • homicide
deduction • forgery • master criminal • suspect • victim • murderer
questioning • incriminate • fingerprint analysis • DNA sample
proof • clue
accomplice
alibi • private eye
evidence
profiling
hunch • forensics
private detective • motive • false identity

AUTHOR SAYS

If you're stuck, look for tips from Christopher Edge, an award-winning children's author.

RED ALERT!

RED ALERT

Need some help with your **spelling**, **grammar**, and **punctuation**? Red alerts give you the lowdown on what you need to know to make your story the best ever.

A clause is part of a sentence that has its own verb.

- A sentence can contain one or more **main clauses**, linked by a conjunction such as **and**, **but**, **or**, or **yet**, or by a semicolon.

- A **subordinate clause** begins with a conjunction such as **because**, **if**, or **when**, and it can come before or after the main clause.

- A **relative clause** explains or describes something that has just been mentioned, and is introduced by **that**, **which**, **who**, **whom**, **whose**, **when**, or **where**.

A short punchy sentence can shock the reader. A longer one can build up suspense.

INSPIRATION STATION

INSPIRATION STATION

Take a page out of some of the best books around and find inspiration from the words of some fantastic children's authors. Try out the techniques they use in your own story.

Using similes and metaphors can add suspense to your story.

Poirot locked the door on the inside, and proceeded to a minute inspection of the room. He darted from one object to another with the agility of a grasshopper. I remained by the door, fearing to obliterate any clues. —THE MYSTERIOUS AFFAIR AT STYLES **by Agatha Christie**

A slight black-coated figure crept into the room like a thief, pausing with every footstep as the tick of the grandfather clock standing in the corner kept time with her thumping heartbeat.
—TWELVE MINUTES TO MIDNIGHT **by Christopher Edge**

STORY SPARKS

Stuck for a story idea? You need a spark of inspiration to set your imagination on fire!

You can find story sparks everywhere—from newspaper headlines such as "ROMAN SOLDIERS MARCH ON BRITAIN'S MOST HAUNTED MOTORWAY" to overheard conversations such as "So I told him if he wanted to be a vampire he had to eat his greens first . . . "

From creepy castles to hi-tech headquarters, places you visit or even just see on TV could inspire the setting for a story. A person you meet or glimpse on the street might give you the idea for a character.

Keep your eyes and ears open to help you discover your own story ideas.

The Language of Genre

A particular style or type of story is called a genre. There are lots of different genres to choose from. Choose from the web below to decide which genre your story idea might fit. You could choose more than one!

autobiography

mystery

romance

Gothic

spy

crime

science fiction

adventure

school

detective

fairy tale

diary

horror

fable

screenplay

thriller

historical

comic book

scary

play

script

animal

myth

fantasy

mash-up

comedy

sports

ghost

Keep a notebook or app on hand to scribble down your story ideas. This might be a word or phrase that catches your eye, a picture that pops into your mind, or just a random thought.

Asking questions can help you to develop your initial idea into the plot of a story. What if my mom could read my mind? How could a kitten beat a grizzly bear in a fight?

You probably won't think up the entire plot of your story at once. Making connections between different ideas, characters, and places can help you to create an original story. Don't worry if you've not mapped out the whole thing. You might not know the ending of your story until you get there!

INSPIRATION STATION

What stories could the following lines inspire?

Today is the one day in the year when all visitors are banned, on pain of death.
— *STRAVAGANZA: CITY OF MASKS*
by Mary Hoffman

By and by there was to be heard a sound at once the most musical and the most melancholy in the world: the mermaids calling to the moon.
— *THE ADVENTURES OF PETER PAN*
by J. M. Barrie

Author says . . .

Give yourself time to daydream. Sometimes ideas for stories pop into your head when you're staring out of the window. If your teacher asks what you're doing tell them you're hard at work thinking up a great story!

Keep a notebook by your bed and write down your dreams when you wake up.

RED ALERT!

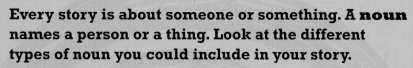

Every story is about someone or something. A noun names a person or a thing. Look at the different types of noun you could include in your story.

- A **proper noun** identifies a particular person, place, or thing. Proper nouns begin with capital letters.
  James   Africa   Friday

- A **common noun** refers to people or things in general.
  dog   treasure   bridge

- A **concrete noun** refers to people and things that can be seen, touched, smelled, heard, or tasted.
  pencil   banana   rain   beach   tune

- An **abstract noun** refers to ideas, qualities, and conditions —things that cannot be seen or touched.
  danger   happiness   friendship

CREATING CHARACTERS

Great stories are about great characters. Creating a character profile can help you to build a picture of the different characters in your story.

Remember, you need to make your characters stand out. Don't confuse readers by making your hero and villain look the same—unless the fact that they're lookalikes is an important part of the plot!

Character Profile

You should decide:
What the character looks like
– do they have any distinguishing features?

How they speak and what they say
– are they a booming loudmouth or a shy whispering mouse?

What they do and what they think
– do their actions speak louder than their thoughts?

What they want and why they want it
– what is their goal and how will they get it?

How other characters react to them
– are they frightened, are they friends, or do they just think they're a fool?

Will your character change in the story
– how might they be different at the end and why?

The Language of Character

Which words from the web could you use to describe the different characters in your story?

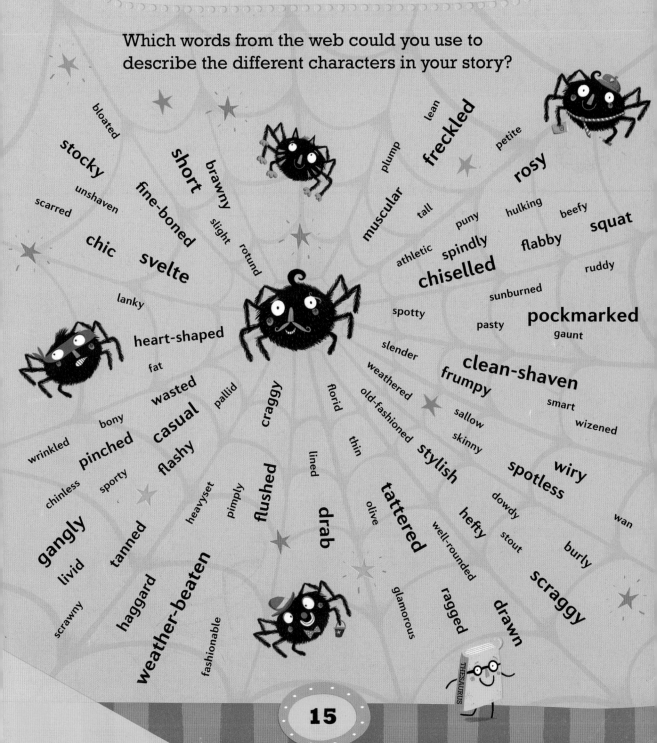

bloated
stocky
scarred
unshaven
short
brawny
fine-boned
slight
rotund
chic
svelte
lanky
heart-shaped
fat
wasted
bony
wrinkled
pinched
chinless
sporty
flashy
casual
pallid
craggy
gangly
livid
tanned
heavyset
pimply
flushed
scrawny
haggard
weather-beaten
fashionable
drab
lined
thin
olive
florid
weathered
old-fashioned
slender
spotty
muscular
plump
lean
freckled
petite
rosy
tall
puny
hulking
beefy
squat
athletic
spindly
flabby
chiselled
ruddy
sunburned
pasty
pockmarked
gaunt
clean-shaven
frumpy
smart
sallow
skinny
wizened
stylish
wiry
spotless
dowdy
tattered
hefty
stout
wan
well-rounded
burly
ragged
drawn
scraggy
glamorous

You need to make your main character the star of the story. Every action they take should move the plot forward. Whether this is standing up to the school bully or leading an army into battle against alien invaders, what your character does should reveal something about who they are.

Think about the strengths and weaknesses you give each character. Does your hero have any flaws such as a secret phobia of spiders? Can you give your villain any positive features, like phoning their grandma every day, to make them a more interesting character?

INSPIRATION STATION

Descriptive details can give the reader an instant impression of a character.

Chudleigh Pomeroy came storming in, his toupee askew and his round face red with indignation.
— MORTAL ENGINES by Philip Reeve

Malfoy gave Professor Lupin an insolent stare, which took in the patches on his robes and the dilapidated suitcase.
— HARRY POTTER AND THE PRISONER OF AZKABAN by J. K. Rowling

Author says . . .

The names you choose can give your readers clues about your characters. How would you expect a character called Queen Tippsy-Wippsy to behave?

What do you think an alien called Glob would look like?

RED ALERT!

An **adjective** gives more information about a noun. You can use adjectives to give more information about the characters in your story.

The little green alien zapped the frightened schoolboy.

The adjectives **little** and **green** give more information about the alien and the adjective **frightened** gives more information about the schoolboy. Remember an adjective usually goes before the noun.

SETTING THE SCENE

Where does your story take place? When does your story happen? Whether you're writing a spy thriller or a fantasy adventure, a science fiction saga or a furry animal tale, the setting you choose will influence the story you tell.

Does your story take place in a real-life location? Take a visit to this place and jot down any details that you could drop into your story. Sights, sounds, smells, and sensations can all help a reader to picture a place.

You can also use online maps and tools to explore anywhere in the world. If your story is set in New York, take a virtual walk down the streets of the Big Apple to spot things that will make your setting seem real to the reader.

The Language of Landscape

Use the words in the web to help you choose the different locations you could use in your story. Think about how your vocabulary can help readers to imagine these places.

airy
loch
tundra
furrowed
steppe
island
grand
plateau
compact
crumbling
ice ridge
sound
rugged
sprawling
irrigated
rocky
wooded
enclosed
steep
hillside
rainforest
rise
crevice
desert
ramshackle
fjord
gorge
exposed
ploughed
cramped
creek
shady
moor
bush
crevasse
pool
sun-drenched
pass
valley
cove
cavern
lowland
barren
crag
geyser
cave
escarpment
arid
farmed
spacious
ledge
imposing
lake
bay
pond
hillock
inlet
peninsula
mountainous
bayou
riverbank
river
stark
levee
ravine
field
run-down
grassland
bleak
rivulet
ruined
path
precipice
water hole
copse
sheltered
gully
range
jagged
wasteland
mountain
glen
lunar
wetland
squalid
patchwork
oasis
fenced
slope
glacier
channel
pitted
inhospitable
beach
savannah
prairie
forest
furrow
hill
ice floe
swamp
craggy
plain
lagoon
bog
stately
dell
dike
bare hilly
fallow
forbidding
wood
waterfall
dam
canal
spring
knoll
ridge
fertile
lush
track
bridge
DICTIONARY
stream
dune
marsh
open

If your story is set in the past, read non-fiction books to find out more about this period and look for photos or paintings to help you picture this time and place.

If you're writing a fantasy or science fiction story, you could make a map of the world that you're creating. From lost mountains to cloud cities, mapping out the journey of your story can give you ideas for exciting new scenes.

INSPIRATION STATION

Weather can reflect a character's mood.

The sky rumbled loudly above them and the rain continued to pour down, bouncing on the lane and running into little streams. — *GOODNIGHT MISTER TOM* by Michelle Magorian

The storm was raging outside. Rain lashed against the windows, the wind howled through the telegraph wires. — *GRANNY NOTHING* by Catherine MacPhail

That summer the sun was a mighty furnace, with a blast so fierce it loosened the edges of things. — *THE OPPOSITE OF CHOCOLATE* by Julie Bertagna

RED ALERT!

A **preposition** shows how things are related. It can describe the position of something, the time when something happens, or the way in which something is done.

The water cascaded **over** the lip of the basin and dropped, in a miniature Niagara Falls, **onto** the kitchen floor.
— *MEASLE AND THE SLITHERGHOUL* by Ian Ogilvy

The prepositions **over** and **onto** show exactly how the water spills from the basin to the floor.

Here are some more prepositions you can use to help your readers picture the settings you describe.
above, against, behind, below, beside, between, in, inside, near, on, off, outside, through, under

Author says . . .

Remember you're writing a story not a travel guide! Look for ways you can weave details about the setting into the action of your story such as, "His fingers scrabbled to find a grip on the crumbling rockface as the assassin took aim again."

Imagine your characters in the setting you've created. What might they be doing there? How will they react?

Try to describe what they can see, hear, and smell.

WHAT'S THE PLOT?

You might have a head full of ideas, but you need to organize them into a plot. A plot is the things that happen in your story, arranged in a logical order.

A story needs a beginning, a middle, and an end. Think about the event that kicks off your story and where you want your characters to be at the close of play.

Now make a list of everything else that happens in your story. Creating a plot is like climbing a mountain—each event or step in your story should build on the one before. There could be twists and turns as the characters face problems or challenges and peaks of excitement as dramatic events take place.

★ Plot ★

Story

✳ Endings ✳

Resolution

Problems

Challenges

Build-up

Beginnings

The Language of Plot

Use the words in the web to help you to think about the structure of your story.

Plot

connections

Beginnings

description

What happens?

mission

setting the scene

introduction

dramatic opening

Build-up

Why does this happen?

setup

catalyst

Story

embarrassing situations

changes

mistaken identity

obstacles

complications

Challenges

difficulties

turning point

climax

pace

mix-ups

crisis

Problems

action

conflict

excitement

twists

confrontation

cliff-hanger

conclusion

untangling

Resolution

Endings

happy ever after

close

THESAURUS

Visualize the plot of your story before you start writing it. You could draw a flow chart with arrows showing how different events link together.

Or, how about using a chart to plot the action of your story? Every spike in the chart could show an event that sends the excitement levels soaring. Try to make the spikes get taller as your story reaches its climax.

INSPIRATION STATION

The turning point in your plot could be a dramatic incident that changes everything.

Mildred muttered the spell under her breath—and Ethel vanished. In her place stood a small pink and grey pig.
— *THE WORST WITCH* by Jill Murphy

By lunchtime, the whole place was a seething mass of men, women, and children all pushing and shoving to get a glimpse of this miraculous fruit.
— *JAMES AND THE GIANT PEACH* by Roald Dahl

Author says . . .

What happens next? What would my characters do now? How will they get out of this situation? Working out the answers to these kinds of questions can help if you get stuck.

Think creatively —sometimes the weirdest idea can give you the right solution.

Maybe introducing a new character could give you the answer.

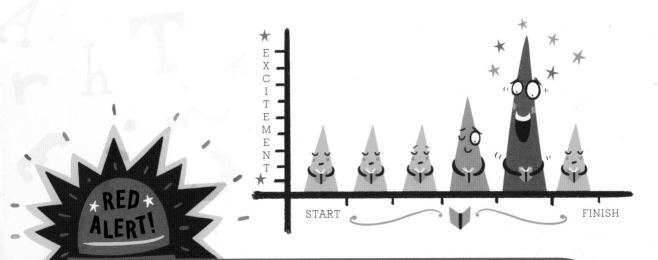

RED ALERT!

A conjunction links clauses, words, or phrases. You can use conjunctions to help you to think about the structure of your story. Link ideas and events together to make sure your plot makes sense.

• A **coordinating conjunction** joins clauses, and other phrases or words that are of the same importance in the sentence.
Lucy thinks the Prime Minister has been kidnapped and tries to rescue him.

Coordinating conjunctions include:
and   but   or   nor   yet

• A **subordinating conjunction** introduces a subordinate clause. A subordinate clause is not as important as the main clause.
The kidnappers chase Lucy because they think she's the Prime Minister's daughter.

Subordinating conjunctions include:
*after   although   as   because   before   for
if   since   so   unless   when   whereas
whether   while   though   until*

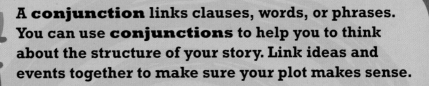

25

STORYTELLING

Who is going to tell your story? Whose voice do you want the reader to hear? You might choose to write from the point of view of one of the characters using the words "I" and "we." This character could be a wisecracking detective, a daring astronaut, or even a booger that's escaped from someone's nose!

Writing in the first person means you describe everything that happens in the story from that character's perspective. Using a first-person narrator can make your story feel very real and exciting. Your readers can share the character's thoughts and feelings.

Think about the words your character would use to bring the story to life through their eyes.

You might even want to tell the same story from the viewpoints of two different characters—this can be a great way to tell a love story!

The Language of Storytelling

If you choose to tell the story in the first person, think about the tone of voice you want to give your narrator.

happy excited eager kind

fresh hurtful obnoxious foolish brave

gentle annoyed sad silly cautious

irritated angry sarcastic resentful bold smart

dull grumpy courageous scared romantic quizzical dreary

secretive cheerful jolly moody

intelligent calm smug sympathetic

mysterious

sinister

embarrassed clever

If you don't want to tell the story from the point of view of one of the characters, you can write in the third person using the words "he," "she," "it" and "they" instead.

If your story has lots of characters and you want to show their different points of view, writing in the third person can let the reader see the story from different angles. You can move between the minds of different characters to show their thoughts and feelings or just describe the thoughts of one character from a third person viewpoint.

Whether you choose to tell the story in the first person or the third person, remember to stick to this. If you switch back and forth between different viewpoints you'll leave your readers' heads spinning.

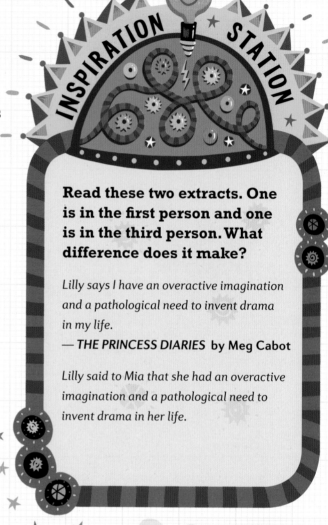

INSPIRATION ★ STATION

Read these two extracts. One is in the first person and one is in the third person. What difference does it make?

Lilly says I have an overactive imagination and a pathological need to invent drama in my life.
— *THE PRINCESS DIARIES* by Meg Cabot

Lilly said to Mia that she had an overactive imagination and a pathological need to invent drama in her life.

Author says . . .

Don't mix up your tenses —in each sentence and your whole story! Try to stick to either the past or present tense to avoid confusing the reader.

Whether it's past or present, choose the tense that works best for your story.

★ RED ★ ALERT!

The **tense** of a verb tells you when the action of the verb takes place. You can choose to write your story in the past or present tense.

- The **present tense** is used to describe something that is happening now. It is usually shown by having no ending, or by adding **-s**.

  Bilbo **climbs** the mountain.
  The dwarves **are** happy.
  The dragon **sniffs** the air.

Using the present tense can make the reader feel as though they're watching the action of the story as it happens.

- The **past tense** is used to describe something that happened earlier. The past tense is usually shown by adding **-ed**.

  Bilbo **climbed** the mountain.
  The dragon **sniffed** the air.

Watch out for verbs which change completely in the past tense.

is ⟶ was   go ⟶ went   think ⟶ thought

STARTING YOUR STORY

A good story should grab your reader's attention from the very first line. This doesn't mean you have to start your story with a huge explosion—although you can if you want to!

A mystery might begin with a dead body being discovered, whereas if you're writing a funny story you want to start with something that will leave your reader in stitches. Whatever type of story you want to tell, try to set the right tone from the very start.

The Language of Openings

Think about how you could change or twist some of these traditional story openings to surprise the reader.

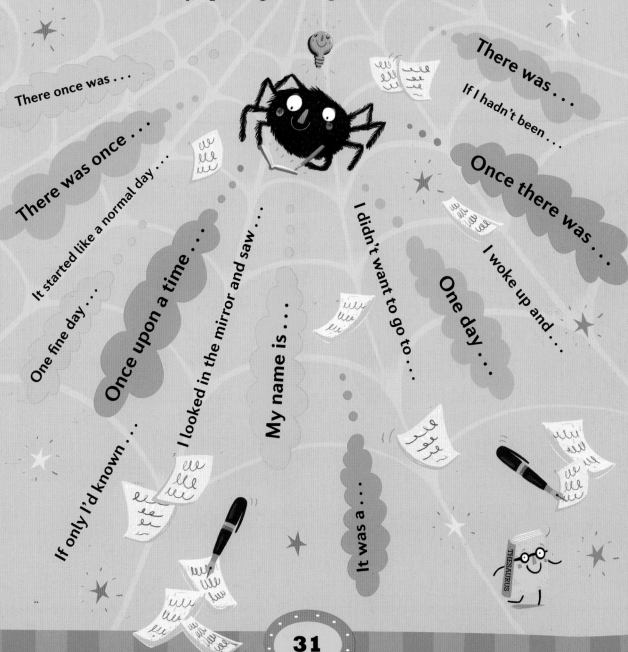

There once was . . .

There was once . . .

It started like a normal day . . .

One fine day . . .

Once upon a time . . .

If only I'd known . . .

I looked in the mirror and saw . . .

My name is . . .

It was a . . . .

I didn't want to go to . . . .

One day . . .

There was . . .

If I hadn't been . . .

Once there was . . .

I woke up and . . .

THESAURUS

There are lots of different ways of starting a story. You could use:

- **description**—introduce characters and the setting of your story,
- **action**—throw your readers into the middle of an exciting event,
- **dialogue**—let the reader hear the characters' voices, or
- an **intriguing question or statement** such as "Beware of the mouse—that's what the sign on the gate said."

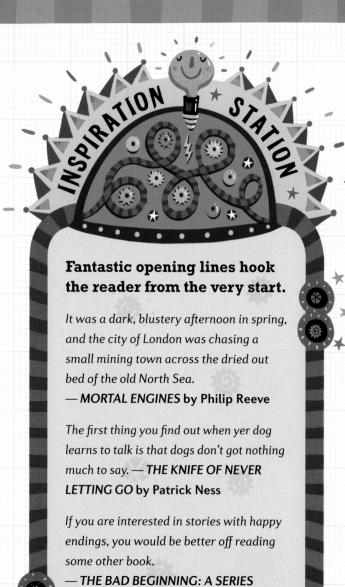

INSPIRATION STATION

Fantastic opening lines hook the reader from the very start.

It was a dark, blustery afternoon in spring, and the city of London was chasing a small mining town across the dried out bed of the old North Sea.
— *MORTAL ENGINES* **by Philip Reeve**

The first thing you find out when yer dog learns to talk is that dogs don't got nothing much to say. — *THE KNIFE OF NEVER LETTING GO* **by Patrick Ness**

If you are interested in stories with happy endings, you would be better off reading some other book.
— *THE BAD BEGINNING: A SERIES OF UNFORTUNATE EVENTS* **by Lemony Snicket**

Author says . . .

However you choose to start your story, make sure this event kick-starts the plot. Get the reader asking questions and keep them turning the pages to find out what happens next.

Don't be afraid to change the start of your story. Keep polishing your opening lines until they shine!

RED ALERT!

Remember to use paragraphs to make your story easy to read and understand.

Start a new paragraph in your story when you are going to start writing about something different such as a different person, location, or event.

ACTION!

If your story has fight scenes, car chases, and huge explosions, getting the action right will make your reader feel like they're watching a blockbuster movie.

Before you start to write an action scene, plan out exactly what's going to happen. You could use action figures or toy cars to choreograph the action or even act it out yourself. This will help you to describe the action in a realistic way.

Don't try to describe every punch or kick—including a few specific details can help the reader to imagine what is happening.

The Language of Action

Think about which verbs you could use to help the reader picture the action. Remember to use the past or present tense form of the verb, depending on how you've chosen to tell your story.

collide lunge crash sidestep

swoop dive

catch hurtle spin pull dash

steal

prod

shoot limp grip turn

fly charge cut wrestle

clash grab dodge

tackle kick collapse fall

evade flinch block jolt explode rush

leap creep yank vault strike soar

zap

accelerate climb hurl stagger skid

drop

chase trip crouch

fight pummel attack destroy

punch

It can be exciting to watch a car chase on the movie screen, but reading pages and pages describing the same car chase will quickly put the reader to sleep. Keep your action scenes short for maximum impact.

Try to avoid any action clichés like your hero walking away from an exploding building without a scratch. Include details that appeal to the reader's senses to help them imagine the experience. You could describe the heat of the blast, the sound of tearing metal, and the unstoppable force of the shockwave. If you get this right, your reader should feel as though they're right in the middle of the action.

ZOOOOM!

INSPIRATION STATION

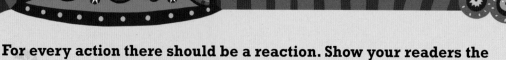

For every action there should be a reaction. Show your readers the impact of the actions you describe.

The next thing Alex knew, the heel of Wolf's palm had rammed into his chest, pushing him back with astonishing force.
— *STORMBREAKER* by Anthony Horowitz

Just as the creature lunged forwards to kill him, Hiccup was grabbed around the ankle by one of Stoick's hairy hands, and pulled back through the hole he had climbed in.
— *HOW TO BE A PIRATE* by Cressida Cowell

RED ALERT!

- Some **verbs** identify an action:
  *The goat **attacked** the troll.*

- Other **verbs** identify thoughts and feelings:
  *The troll **wondered** why the goat was picking on him.*

- Many verbs can be either **active** or **passive**. With an **active verb**, the subject is often who or what does something.
  *The troll **cleans** his cave every week.*

- With a **passive verb**, the focus is on what happens, rather than who does something.
  *The troll's cave **is cleaned** every week.*

- Using active verbs can help you to make your story more dynamic.

Author says . . .

Every action scene you include should move the plot of your story forward. Don't just include a fight to give your characters something to do!

MAKING IT REAL

A picture is worth a thousand words, but if you choose the right words you can help your readers to imagine a cast of a thousand characters, visualize places they've never seen before, and bring the world of your story to life.

Don't just describe what you want the reader to see. If your hero is drugged with a poison, what does it taste like? Think about the other senses you can use to create effective descriptions.

The Language of Description

Use the words in the web to help you describe **sounds**, **smells**, **tastes**, and **sensations**. If you can't find the right one, make it up yourself!

Imagine you're directing a film as you write each scene of your story. Think about how you could move the camera around to help the reader to picture the scene.

You could describe a crowd of thousands in a single line and then switch to a close-up to describe a tear rolling down the face of your hero.

INSPIRATION STATION

Similes can focus the reader on specific details that the writer wants them to imagine.

The building looked like a fiery ghost, with great bursts of flame coming from the windows. — **A SERIES OF UNFORTUNATE EVENTS** by Lemony Snicket

"A bad idea, Professor Lockhart," said Snape, gliding over like a large and malevolent bat. — **HARRY POTTER AND THE CHAMBER OF SECRETS** by J. K. Rowling

At last with a glorious swoop like the dive of a wild sea-bird, the witch and her broomstick came down on the Hurricane Mountains.
— **GOBBOLINO THE WITCH'S CAT** by Ursula Moray Williams

Author says . . .

Use metaphors and similes to help you to describe things in interesting and unusual ways. What would a "moon-skulled" person look like?

How would someone who walked like a huge awkward chicken move?

RED ALERT!

Synonyms are words that mean the same or nearly the same as each other, such as **enormous** and **huge**, or **horrid** and **nasty**.

- Using **synonyms** can help you to avoid repeating the same words in your story.

- **Antonyms** are words that mean the opposite of each other, such as **quick** and **slow**. You can change the meaning of many words by adding a prefix such as **un-**, **im-** or **dis-** at the start of the word, such as **unhappy**, **impossible**, **disliked**, or changing the suffix at the end of the word, such as **careless** and **careful**.

- Using **antonyms** can help you to contrast different things in your story.

TALK THE TALK

Can you put words into somebody else's mouth? Dialogue is what the characters in your story say.

You want to make your characters sound believable, but this doesn't mean they should speak in the same way as people do in real life. If you listen to any conversation you'll hear lots of "ums" and "ers," but you'd soon bore the readers of your story if you include these whenever your characters talk!

Think about how different characters in your story speak. You could help the reader recognize who's talking by giving your villain an annoying catchphrase or making your heroine's best friend always speak in a sarcastic tone.

I'LL BE BACK !

The Language of Dialogue

Most of the time "said" is the only verb you will need to describe who is speaking in your story. The speech verbs in this web should only be used if they add something to your story.

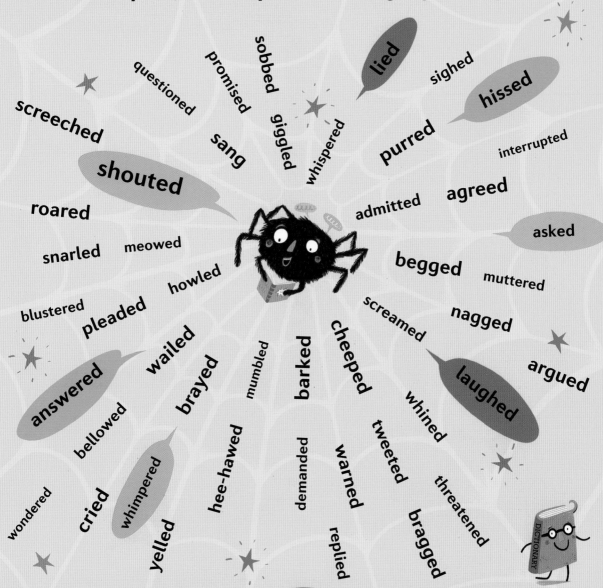

questioned
promised
sobbed
lied
sighed
giggled
whispered
purred
hissed
screeched
sang
shouted
interrupted
admitted
agreed
roared
asked
snarled
meowed
begged
muttered
howled
screamed
nagged
blustered
pleaded
wailed
cheeped
laughed
argued
answered
brayed
mumbled
barked
whined
bellowed
tweeted
wondered
cried
whimpered
hee-hawed
demanded
warned
threatened
bragged
yelled
replied

Think about what you want the characters in your story to say. You can use dialogue to:

- **move the plot of your story forward**—perhaps you could drop a clue to a mystery into a conversation

- **reveal something about the characters in your story**—what a character says and how they say it can show what they think and how they are feeling.

Remember people don't always say what they mean and the same should be true for the characters in your story too . . .

INSPIRATION STATION

Adjectives and adverbs can be used to provide information about the way a character speaks.

"Stupid things!" Alice began in a loud, indignant voice. — *ALICE'S ADVENTURES IN WONDERLAND* **by Lewis Carroll**

"What's the matter?" asked Sorrel sarcastically, venturing so close to the edge of the chasm that her furry toes were over empty space. "Don't you like mountains?" — *DRAGON RIDER* **by Cornelia Funke**

RED ALERT!

When you are writing dialogue in your story, you need to remember to:

- put inverted quotation marks around the words spoken

- use single (' ') or double (" ") quotation marks but keep them consistent

- start a new paragraph whenever the speaker changes

- only include the exact words the speaker says inside the quotation marks

- put punctuation marks inside the quotation marks

- give the name of the person speaking when this would make it clearer for the reader.

Author says . . .

Try to make the different characters in the story sound like individuals. Reread their dialogue, but cover up each character's name.

If you can't tell which character is speaking you might need to change the dialogue.

When your characters speak you want your readers to listen, so make every word of dialogue count.

CREATIVE VOCABULARY

The words you use can help your story come to life in the mind of the reader. Get creative with the vocabulary you choose to create characters, settings, and scenes that they will never forget.

Remember the best word to use isn't always the longest one. If you want to use "hippomonstrosesquippedaliophobia" or "floccinaucinihilipilification" make sure that they make sense in your story!

Weird and Wonderful Vocabulary

Can you use any of the words in the web in your story?
Make sure you understand what the word means before you try!

turgid
gilded
arcane
dormant
hewn
acrid
nefarious

culinary
harrowing • cretaceous • amorphous
corpulent • oaken • chromatic • fathomless
mellifluous • parsimonious
disconsolate • lachrymose • pivotal • sumptuous
bereft • apotropaic

rancid • cordial • mercenary • herbaceous • caliginous

tumultuous • sibilant

crocodilian
labyrinthine
indolent
melodious
bodacious
predatorial • ominous • amphibious
rapacious • ephemeral

pulchritudinous • unadorned • sonorous
omnipotent
stentorian
rambunctious
dauntless
vulpine • ominous
paradoxical
herbaceous
ostentatious

Use your imagination to build your own words. You could invent a new fear such as "mathstestaphobia" or create a dinosaur known as the "Ugliasaurus."

Adding new words or phrases to suffixes such as "-phobia" or "-saurus" can add interesting ideas and characters to your story.

You can also create new words by blending two words to create a compound word.

Your "sleep-fogged" hero might be "terror-stricken" as he wakes to find a "saliva-cobwebbed" spectre looming "wraith-like" above him!

Think about how you can blend different words together to create an original image in the reader's mind.

KAZO

INSPIRATION STATION

The right word can give the reader more information about a character or situation.

Dr. Dandiffer is an ethnobotanist. His speciality is the medicinal use of tropical plants. — *TIME STOPS FOR NO MOUSE* by Michael Hoeye

Quite a hullabaloo was breaking out upstairs, and most of the sounds were by no means pleasant. — *THE WEIRDSTONE OF BRISINGAMEN* by Alan Garner

OOOM!

Author says . . .

Don't always use the first word that comes into your mind. Instead of saying that a character in your story talks a lot, why not describe them as a "blatherskite" or say that they're speaking "loquaciously?"

You can find exciting vocabulary in lots of different places: blockbuster films, TV shows, songs, apps, and video games.

Keep an ear to the ground to steal new words for your story.

Chirp!

RED ALERT!

Onomatopoeia is when the sound of a word imitates what it describes, such as **bang, chirp, buzz,** and **clang.** Using onomatopoeia can help the reader to hear the sounds you describe in your story.

THE END

Every great story needs a great ending. You want to wrap up the plot in a way that leaves the reader satisfied.

Whether it's your hero solving the mystery, finding lost treasure, or triumphing in a final battle against a fire-breathing dragon, any problems or challenges you've introduced in your story should be resolved before you write "The End."

You could give your story a twist ending. This might reveal a secret that a character has kept hidden or surprise the reader with an unexpected event.

Remember your final plot twist needs to make sense, so think about how you can drop hints earlier in the story to build up to this surprise ending.

The Language of Mood

What emotions do you want the reader to feel when they finish the story? Use the words in the web to help you to think about the mood you want to create in your closing scene.

jealous

hopeful

shocked

awed

infuriated

giggly

tense

amused

satisfied

curious

surprised

bewildered

scared

scared to go to sleep

blissful

crushed

nerve-jangled

annoyed

inspired

excited

confused

amused

enraged

cheerful

touched

anxious

pleased

sympathetic

overwhelmed

gloomy

sentimental

drained

enthralled

sad

angry

weird

optimistic

exhilarated

thoughtful

ecstatic

calm

happy

aggravated

THESAURUS

You could link the ending of your story back to the beginning. Perhaps your main character arrives back at the place they started from.

The ending could show how characters have been changed by the events of the story—a cowardly hobbit could now be a brave hero or a school bully turned into a best friend. Think about the ways in which the characters in your story have changed and how you can show this in the end.

Remember, not every story has to end "happily ever after." A cliff-hanger ending can leave your readers in suspense, but this works best if you're planning to carry on the action in a follow-up story.

INSPIRATION STATION

Fantastic final lines stay with a reader long after they've put the story down.

I am haunted by humans.
— *THE BOOK THIEF* by Markus Zusak

The scar had not pained Harry for nineteen years. All was well. — *HARRY POTTER AND THE DEATHLY HALLOWS* by J. K. Rowling

Light falls through the window, falls onto me, into me. Moments. All gathering towards this one.
— *BEFORE I DIE* by Jenny Downham

HOME!

RED ALERT!

An **ellipsis** is a set of three dots used to show that a word has been omitted or a sentence not finished. You can use an ellipsis to indicate a cliff-hanger ending.

Suddenly, the door opened . . .

Author says . . .

Try not to disappoint your readers with a clichéd ending where your character wakes up to discover the story was just a dream.

Think of different ways you could end your story.

Take a look at any books that you love to see how these stories end.

Try to come up with a great last line that your reader will always remember.

CHOOSING A TITLE

You shouldn't judge a book by its cover, but choosing the right title can encourage readers to pick up your story. Try to think of an attention-grabbing title to make your story stand out.

The title you choose could give the reader a hint about what the story will be about. It might tell them:

- what type of story it is—is it an adventure, a romance, a mystery, or a mash-up?
- something about the main character or setting—*Alice in Wonderland* tells you about both!
- something about the ideas and events in the story—*Stop in the Name of Pants!* suggests that this story has something to do with a pair of pants . . .

INSPIRATION STATION

What do you think the following stories are about? What type of story would you expect to read?

Twelve Minutes to Midnight

The World of Norm: May Contain Nuts

MONKEY WARS

My Best Friend and Other Enemies

The Whizz Pop Chocolate Shop

SOLDIER DOG

Author says . . .

You might think of a title before you start to write your story or still be scratching your head for one after you've written the last line.

You could choose a one-word title like "Vanished" or a long title like "The Day I Swapped My Dad for Two Goldfish."

If you're still stuck, flip through the story to see if you can spot any interesting words or phrases that could give you a title with reader-appeal.

IS IT FINISHED?

So you think you've finished your story? Before you rush to put it on the shelf of your local bookstore, take a break instead. Go for a walk, eat a few of your favorite cookies, or just dance around your room all day. Giving your mind a rest from your story will mean you'll be able to spot improvements you can make when you read it again.

Does the plot make sense? Are there any loose ends you've forgotten to tie up? Don't leave your heroine dangling off the edge of the cliff in one scene and then show her sipping a fruit juice on the beach in the next without explaining how she escaped from certain death!

The Language of Editing

Use the questions in the web to help you to check and revise your story.

Are there any scenes that don't move the plot forward?

Does the characters in the story seem real?

Does the pace of the story move fast enough to keep the reader's interest?

Can you tell which characters are speaking when you read their dialogue?

Does the opening of the story grab the reader's attention?

Can you picture the settings described?

You need to make sure that readers will be able to understand every part of your story.

Check that what you have written is clear and accurate, with periods and capital letters in the correct places. Look out for any errors that you know you tend to make in your writing.

Once you've made any final revisions to your story, why not show it to a friend to get a second opinion? Sometimes a fresh pair of eyes can spot any mistakes you've missed. Choose a friend who likes the type of story you've written and ask if they can suggest any improvements you can make.

When you're happy with your finished story, share it with as many readers as you can. You could keep your eyes peeled for any short story competitions you can enter.

You're never too young to make it big in books. The best-selling author, Christopher Paolini was only fifteen when he started writing his fantasy story *Eragon* which has now sold millions of copies and been made into a blockbuster film.

DICTIONARY

Beginnings

Story

Resolution

Plot

THESAURUS

Endings

Build-up

Problems

Challenges

Author says . . .

Try to avoid clichés and clumsy phrases and don't be afraid to make changes. If in doubt, cut it out!

Reading your story out loud can help you spot anything that doesn't sound right.

You can use a spell-checker but your dictionary and thesaurus can give you lots of extra information too.

RED ALERT!

Check the spelling in your story to make sure you haven't mixed up any of these commonly confused words:

- **clothes** are things that you wear ⟶ **cloths** are pieces of material you use to wipe a table

- **nether** means low down or lower ⟶ **never** means not ever or not at all ⟶ **neither** means not either

- **collage** is a picture made by sticking small objects to a surface ⟶ **college** is a place where people go to learn after they have left school

- **exited** means to leave a place ⟶ **excited** means to feel eager or enthusiastic about something

How to Write Your Best
ADVENTURE STORY Ever!

When you write an adventure story you want to send your reader on a journey into the unknown. This might be a search for ancient treasure or a long-lost land.

Start your story with a dramatic event that pulls your hero or heroine out of their everyday life and plunges them headfirst into adventure.

What type of personality will you give your hero or heroine? Will they show courage to conquer the dangers they face and use their imagination to escape from tricky situations? Or will they be jokers who stumble and bumble their way into an adventure? Show their personality in the way you describe their actions and behavior.

The Language of Adventure

You could use some of this adventurous vocabulary in your story.

heist action danger map challenging exciting

abandon quest

bandit villain sabotage island

loot fortune

jewels bold exploit ruthless prowl revenge intrepid sword ferocious outcast greed

corpse fear evil escapade criminal enemy

gold violence weapons gun embark legend thrills

notorious hostile horizon fight knife

eventful escape treasure venture daring attack discover

Location, location, location. From ruined temples to dense jungles, dark caverns to perilous shipwrecks, the setting for your adventure story needs to be a dangerous place where twists and turns can surprise your main character.

Maybe you could give the hero of your story a sidekick. Think about this character's strengths and weaknesses and how they could help or hinder your hero along the way.

Your story could also include an antagonist—a rival for your hero, who's chasing after the same goal. Will your hero achieve the aim of their adventure or could the antagonist triumph in the end?

INSPIRATION STATION

The nouns and verbs you choose can help you to create a distinctive setting.

Beyond the woods and the strawberry fields, the Long Island Sound glittered in the last light of the sun. — PERCY JACKSON AND THE LIGHTNING THIEF **by Rick Riordan**

The Nautilus had put on full speed. All the quiet lustre of the ice-walls was at once changed into flashes of lightning. —20,000 LEAGUES UNDER THE SEA **by Jules Verne**

Author says . . .

Think about any adventurous places you have visited or seen to help you to find inspiration for the setting of your adventure story.

Films, TV shows, or computer games you play can all give you ideas for fantastic settings.

RED ALERT!

An **adverb** is a word that adds to the meaning of a verb, adjective, or another adverb. Would you use any of these **adverbs** to describe the actions of your hero?

loquaciously (loquacious = talkative)

lugubriously (lugubrious = gloomy or mournful)

scintillatingly (scintillating = 1. to give off sparks or flashes of light
= 2. to be lively or witty)

Choose your own unusual adverbs to help describe your hero/heroine as he/she embarks on the adventure. You can use an adverb with an adjective to liven up descriptions.

violently hot trifle, **gently** springy grass, **scarily** serious situation

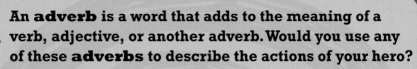

How to Write Your Best
MYSTERY STORY Ever!

From Gorgonzola-thieving mice to murdered aristocrats, any puzzling problem or sinister crime could make the perfect starting point for your story. Use your imagination to give your readers a riddle that they'll be desperate to solve.

You'll need to create an investigator to follow the trail of clues in your story. Don't just settle for any secondhand Sherlock Holmes character—try to think up a detective with a difference that your readers will root for. This might be a schoolgirl sleuth armed with a mystery-solving app or even a crime-fighting baby who googles for clues!

The Language of Crime

Could you weave any of these words into your mystery story?

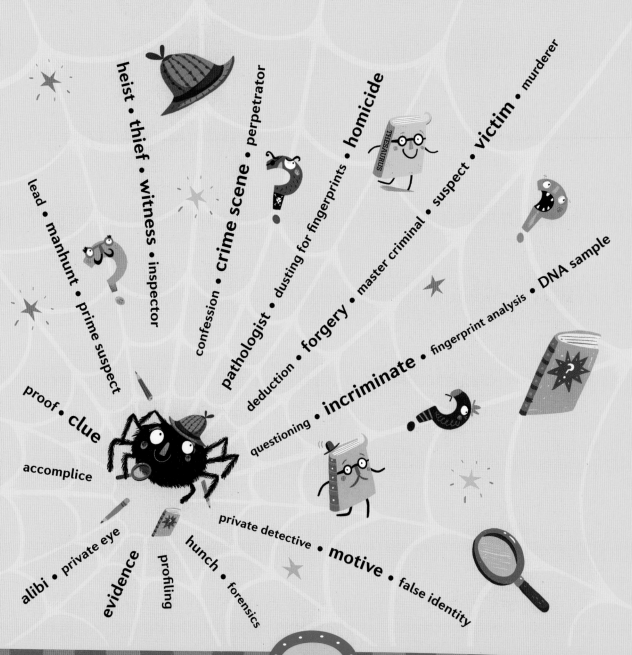

heist • thief • witness • inspector

perpetrator • crime scene • confession

pathologist • dusting for fingerprints • homicide

suspect • master criminal • victim • murderer

deduction • forgery • incriminate • fingerprint analysis • DNA sample

lead • manhunt • prime suspect

proof • clue

accomplice

questioning

private detective • motive • false identity

alibi • private eye • evidence • profiling • hunch • forensics

Next on your character list should be any suspects you want to put in the frame. Teachers, celebrities, butlers, and beasts: who could be the villain hiding in the shadows?

Will you solve the mystery or could there be a twist at the end of your tale? Try to keep your readers guessing until the very last line of your story.

INSPIRATION STATION

Using similes and metaphors can add suspense to your story.

Poirot locked the door on the inside, and proceeded to a minute inspection of the room. He darted from one object to another with the agility of a grasshopper. I remained by the door, fearing to obliterate any clues. —**THE MYSTERIOUS AFFAIR AT STYLES** by Agatha Christie

A slight black-coated figure crept into the room like a thief, pausing with every footstep as the tick of the grandfather clock standing in the corner kept time with her thumping heartbeat. —**TWELVE MINUTES TO MIDNIGHT** by Christopher Edge

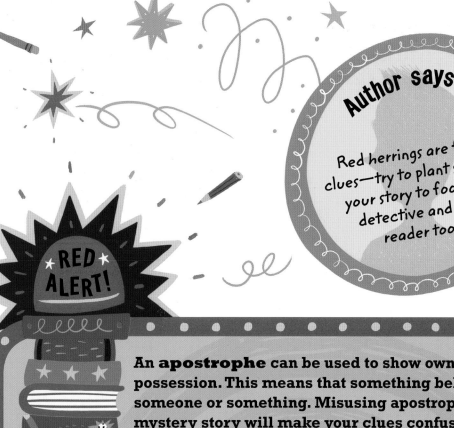

Author says . . .

Red herrings are false clues—try to plant some in your story to fool the detective and the reader too.

RED ALERT!

An **apostrophe** can be used to show ownership or possession. This means that something belongs to someone or something. Misusing apostrophes in a mystery story will make your clues confusing.

Follow these rules to get it right.

- If a singular word doesn't end in **-s**, add **'s**:
  It was the victim's pen.

- If a singular word ends in **-s**, add either **'s** or just **'**:
  It was James's hat. No, it was Nicholas' hat.

- If a singular word ends in **-ss**, still add **'s**:
  I didn't hear the witness's statement.

- If a plural ends in **-s**, just add **'**:
  The marks were left by the calves' horns.

- If a plural doesn't end in **-s**, add **'s**:
  The women's shoes were all red.

How to Write Your Best SCARY STORY Ever!

What scares you? A haunted house with creaking stairs? A ghostly apparition flitting through the forest? A vampire rising from its grave as the clock strikes twelve?

When writing a scary story you can turn your own fears into fiction and give your readers a fright!

You could take the usual scary suspects such as ghosts and zombies, werewolves and monsters, and give them a new direction to create your own spine-chilling tale. Or perhaps you could add a supernatural twist to an ordinary object or situation, such as a cursed smartphone with an app that can bring the dead back to life . . .

The Language of Horror

Which words from the web could you use to describe the **characters**, **settings**, and **events** of your **scary** story?

poisonous
howl
creak
hover
scare
haunt
night
moon
spell
dark
creepy
mouldy
petrify
shiver
terror
gasp
wail
evil
magical
horrible
weird
dismal
wicked
beast
cave
scared
terrifying
spirit
dread
scary
vanish
murky
moan
dusty
scream
dungeon
cemetery
graveyard
dark side
trance
gore
shroud
dead
afraid
diabolical
haunted mansion
mausoleum
tomb
crypt
ghoulish
paranormal
apparition
coffin
ghostly
spectral
supernatural
beyond the grave
poltergeist
zombie
ghost
phantom
necromancer
ghoul
wraith
ghost-hunter
mummy
werewolf
vampire-slayer
uncanny
vampire
necropolis
spectre
afterlife
other-worldly
catacombs
unearthly
corpse
soul
eerie
accursed
curse
living dead
Halloween
macabre
nightmare
undead
hex
afterlife

If you want to give the reader maximum chills, try to write in a way that makes them feel as though they're stuck inside your scary story.

Include spooky details that appeal to their five senses—sight, hearing, smell, touch, and taste. This might be the sound of shuffling footsteps and the shiver of an ice-cold breath on the back of your heroine's neck as she sits in an empty room . . .

Build up the tension in your tale by dropping in these creepy details at the right time for maximum fright effect and let your readers' imaginations do the rest!

Do you want to create a creepy scene or frighten your readers with some gore?

The ghosts clambered out of the earth, pale forms paler still in the midday light.
— *THE AMBER SPYGLASS* by Philip Pullman

And then, as her face contorted into a horrible shape, she bared her fangs, burying them swiftly into his neck.
— *BUFFY THE VAMPIRE-SLAYER: THE HARVEST* by Joss Whedon

The howling is horrendous, a terrible baying noise, blocking out all other sounds, filling us up, tipping us towards madness. — *WHISPERS IN THE GRAVEYARD* by Theresa Breslin

Author says . . .

Think about the pace of your story. You could use a slow pace to build suspense and then shock the reader with a scary event.

Make your reader care about the characters in your story.

If they're rooting for the heroine, your reader will be even more frightened when the monster looms behind them . . .

RED ALERT!

A **cliché** is a phrase that is used so often that it loses its impact. Try to avoid any of these clichés and use more original phrases instead.

I was quaking in my boots.

He stood frozen to the spot.

She was trembling like a leaf.

My hair stood on end.

How to Write Your Best
FUNNY STORY Ever!

Think funny. If you can make your friends laugh, then you're halfway there to giving your readers giggles on the page. Eccentric characters, silly situations, and embarrassing moments can all be used to cook up a side-splitting story.

Whether it's a gangster banana being chased by a police pigeon or your headteacher wearing fifty pairs of underpants on his head—take whatever idea you choose and think about how you can make it even funnier.

From a banana's bad day to a school fashion show disaster, try to develop your original idea into the plot of a laugh-out-loud story.

Make a list of the most embarrassing things that have ever happened to you. Could you turn any of these into a comic scene in your story?

The Language of Comedy

Get inventive with your vocabulary to add humor to your story. Make sure you understand what the word means before you use it to get a laugh!

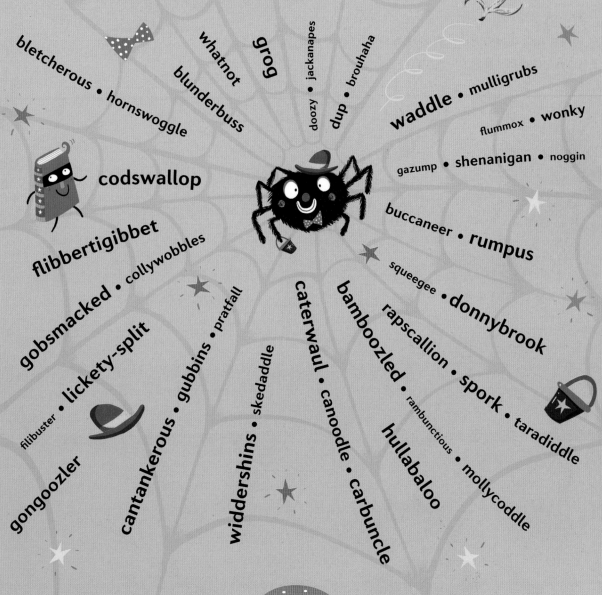

bletcherous • hornswoggle

whatnot

blunderbuss

grog

doozy • jackanapes

dup • brouhaha

waddle • mulligrubs

flummox • wonky

gazump • shenanigan • noggin

codswallop

buccaneer • rumpus

squeegee • donnybrook

flibbertigibbet

gobsmacked • collywobbles

rapscallion • spork • taradiddle

rambunctious • mollycoddle

filibuster • lickety-split

gubbins • pratfall

caterwaul

bamboozled

hullabaloo

gongoozler

cantankerous

widdershins • skedaddle

canoodle • carbuncle

The way you tell your story can add to the humor. If you're writing in the first person, think about how your main character will describe the things that happen to them.

Will they stay upbeat even when they're stuck in an embarrassing situation or do they see everything as a total disaster?

INSPIRATION STATION

Take a page out of Roald Dahl's books to create your own fantastically funny similes.

As she floated gently down, Mrs Twit's petticoat billowed out like a parachute, showing her long knickers.
— **THE TWITS by Roald Dahl**

Suddenly the boy let out a gigantic belch which rolled around the Assembly Hall like thunder.
— **MATILDA by Roald Dahl**

Aunt Sponge, fat and pulpy as a jellyfish, came waddling up behind her sister to see what was going on. — **JAMES AND THE GIANT PEACH by Roald Dahl**

Author says . . .

Sometimes the best funny characters have a unique way of looking at the world. Try to put yourselves in their shoes as you write the story.

Does the heroine of your story always say or do the wrong thing?

If what you write makes you laugh, the chances are your readers will, too!

RED ALERT!

A hyphen can be used to join two or more words to create a new word. Think of the words you could combine to make some pants-splittingly funny new words.

Hyphens are also useful for making your meaning clear.

If you write "a man eating tiger" this could be a man eating a tiger.

If you add a hyphen and write "a man-eating tiger" this shows that it is a tiger that eats men. Forgetting a hyphen can be a dangerous mistake to make!

How to Write Your Best
FANTASY STORY Ever!

Got a head full of dragons, wizards, and fairies but don't know how to turn them into a story? Giving your characters a quest to follow can help you turn your fantastical ideas into fantastic fantasy fiction.

Some heroes set off in search of magical treasures or mysterious lands, while others battle to slay dragons or defeat evil wizards. Whatever quest you choose, think about the trials and traps you could set for your characters along the way. The greater the danger, the faster your readers will turn the pages to find out what happens next.

The Language of Fantasy

Use the words from the web to help you create fabulous **quests**, characters, and **settings**.

witchcraft
spell
elixir
staff
prophecy
legend
lore
alchemist
faerie
sorcerer
enchantress
boggart
banshee
changeling
ogre
bewitched
omen
magic
amulet
rune
curse
shape-shifter
enchanter
cyclops
warlock
basilisk
chronicle
charm
incantation
nemesis
talisman
mermaid
genie
gorgon
merman
hex
invisibility
oracle
wizardry
potion
riddle
vision
dwarf
elf
centaur
selkie
giant
harpie
unicorn
wizard
phoenix
fairy
portal
wand
immortality
enchantment
mace
sorcery
goblin
witch
kelpie
troll
druid
sorceress
dragon

maze
kingdom
cavern
castle
underworld
den
empire
enchanted forest
fortress
stronghold
dungeon
realm
island
lair
cave
labyrinth

77

Even if you are creating a fantasy world filled with magic and monsters, you still need to make your readers believe it is real.

Make a map to help you to understand the place where your story is set and think about what rules this world has.

Do dragons speak? Can wizards fly? Deciding on the rules can help you work out what could happen in your story.

INSPIRATION STATION

Carefully chosen adjectives help readers imagine the world of the story.

Dark and deeply mysterious, the Deepwoods is a harsh and perilous place for those who call it home.
— ***BEYOND THE DEEP WOODS***
by Paul Stewart and Chris Riddell

The island of Gont, a single mountain that lifts its peak a mile above the storm-racked Northeast Sea, is a land famous for wizards.
— ***A WIZARD OF EARTHSEA***
by Ursula Le Guin

RED ALERT!

Archaic words and spellings are ones which were used in the past, such as **faerie**, **daemon**, **vampyre**, and **mage.** Can you find out any other archaic words or spellings you could use in your fantasy story?

Author says . . .

You can use ideas and vocabulary from fantasy books you have read or films that you've seen. This could be wands from Hogwarts, orcs from Middle-Earth, and witches from Narnia.

Give these ideas a twist to make them your own.

How to Write Your Best
SCIENCE FICTION STORY Ever!

Want to take your readers on a journey to alien worlds, let them travel in time, or even make them face a robot apocalypse? Writing a science fiction story lets you imagine what the future might look like.

You don't need an alien mega-mind to come up with story ideas. Asking "What if . . . ?" questions is a great way of thinking up a science fiction plot. What if every robot in the world went rogue? What if the new kid in school turned out to be an alien?

The Language of Science Fiction

Zap words from the web into your story to help you create a tale that is out of this world.

unidentified flying object

DNA

ET

galactical

extraterrestrial

cyborg

rocky   spacecraft

robot

humanoid

airless

portal

icy

paradoxical

force-field

volcanic

hyperspace

uninhabitable

space station

starship

noxious

teleport

spaceship

thin

earthling

clone

outer space

dusty

Earth-like

desolate

frozen

android

molten

spliced

barren

alien

UFO

gaseous

inhospitable

poisonous

unbreathable

THESAURUS

81

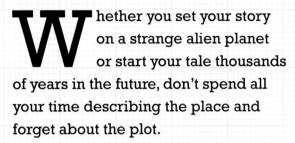

Whether you set your story on a strange alien planet or start your tale thousands of years in the future, don't spend all your time describing the place and forget about the plot.

Drop your characters into the action and let your readers discover more about the futuristic world you've invented as the story unfolds.

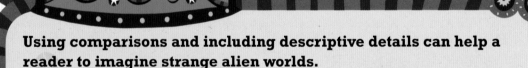

INSPIRATION STATION

Using comparisons and including descriptive details can help a reader to imagine strange alien worlds.

What lay before him looked at first strangely like an earthly landscape—a landscape of grey downland ridges rising and falling likes waves of the sea. — *OUT OF THE SILENT PLANET* by C. S. Lewis

I am told the ground shook, that the skies were full of light and explosions. We were in that two- *week period of the year when both moons hang on opposite sides of the horizon.* — *I AM NUMBER FOUR* by Pittacus Lore

Those who have never seen a living Martian can scarcely imagine the strange horror of its appearance. — *THE WAR OF THE WORLDS* by H. G. Wells

Author says . . .

From creating clones to sending a mission to Mars, think about the amazing discoveries scientists have made to inspire your own story.

Remember science fiction stories can be about what life is like today not just tomorrow.

Think about the world around you —what problems and challenges could be solved by science fiction?

RED ALERT!

Science fiction can be about new inventions, alien planets, and future worlds, so get inventing some new vocabulary and think up the words we'll be using in the Year 3000! Try some of these to get you started:

zaporlazer   invisiblotron   bullyborg

geekbot   teleportal   electropaper

worldominationator   galactaspectacles

spectrominator   robo-mouse

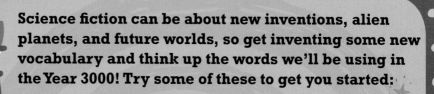

How to Write Your Best
SPY STORY Ever!

Deadly assassins, rogue secret agents, teenage cyber-spies —when the fate of the world is at stake, you need to create a spy who can save the day.

Think about the skills and characteristics you want to give your hero or heroine. Maybe she's a daring martial arts expert who cracks jokes in the face of danger or perhaps he's an accident-prone spy with the nickname, Double Oh No! Whatever you choose, this character should be at the heart of the action.

Start your story with a bang to grab the reader's attention. Perhaps your hero could foil a plot to blow up the Houses of Parliament or deactivate a robot assassin who has got the Prime Minister in his sights.

The Language of Espionage

The world of spying has its own vocabulary. Use the words from the web to create shadowy characters and plots.

MI5
clandestine
briefing
controller
defection
FBI
behind enemy lines
clandestine operation
mole
debriefing
deep cover
secret agent
encode
secret service
covert
code book
spying
encryption
intelligence
surveillance
counter-espionage
double agent
disinformation
code-maker
spymaster
headquarters
infiltration
mission
counter-intelligence
operative
transmitting device
MI6
decode
cryptographer
agent
password
CIA
false identity
sleeper
under cover
NSA
decryption
spy catcher
espionage
hidden camera
recruitment
homeland security
special operations
cipher

Every spy story needs a villain. Try to avoid clichéd baddies like a mad scientist plotting to destroy the world with his death ray. Give your villain a motive for his or her sinister plans.

An exciting mix of action, plot twists, and cliff-hangers will keep your readers turning the pages. Perhaps your heroine could be betrayed by someone she thinks is a friend or escape from certain death by the skin of her teeth.

At the end of the story, your main character should confront the big bad villain and face the ultimate danger as they try to put a stop to their evil scheme.

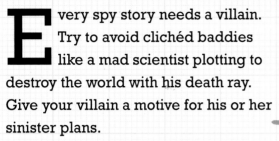

INSPIRATION STATION

Showing characters' emotions can build the tension.

Alex sat hunched up in the back of the low-flying C-130 military aircraft, his stomach churning behind his knees.
— *STORMBREAKER* by Anthony Horowitz

The jeep inched forward at a painfully slow rate, made all the more excruciating by the anticipation building in Artemis's chest.
— *ARTEMIS FOWL* by Eoin Colfer

Author says . . .

Why not create a spy with a difference? You could write a story about Marrowbone Bond, secret agent at the Canine Spy Service who is trying to stop an evil fluffy white cat from taking over the world.

The greater the danger, the higher the excitement. Try to come up with a plot that will keep your reader on the edge of their seat.

RED ALERT!

A clause is part of a sentence that has its own verb.

- A sentence can contain one or more **main clauses**, linked by a conjunction such as **and**, **but**, **or**, or **yet**, or by a semicolon.

- A **subordinate clause** begins with a conjunction such as **because**, **if**, or **when**, and it can come before or after the main clause.

- A **relative clause** explains or describes something that has just been mentioned, and is introduced by **that**, **which**, **who**, **whom**, **whose**, **when**, or **where**.

A short punchy sentence can shock the reader.
A longer one can build up suspense.

How to Write Your Best
LOVE STORY Ever!

Boy meets girl. Robot meets cyborg. Beauty meets beast. Before you can start writing your love story, you've got to decide who's going to fall in love!

Think about how your lead characters might meet and what they will think of each other at first. Will it be love at first sight or will they start the story hating each other?

Remember the course of true love should never run smoothly. What obstacles could you place in the paths of your star-crossed couple?

To make a great love story, your characters must be able to conquer any problem that keeps them apart.

The Language of Love

Could you use any of these words in your romantic story?

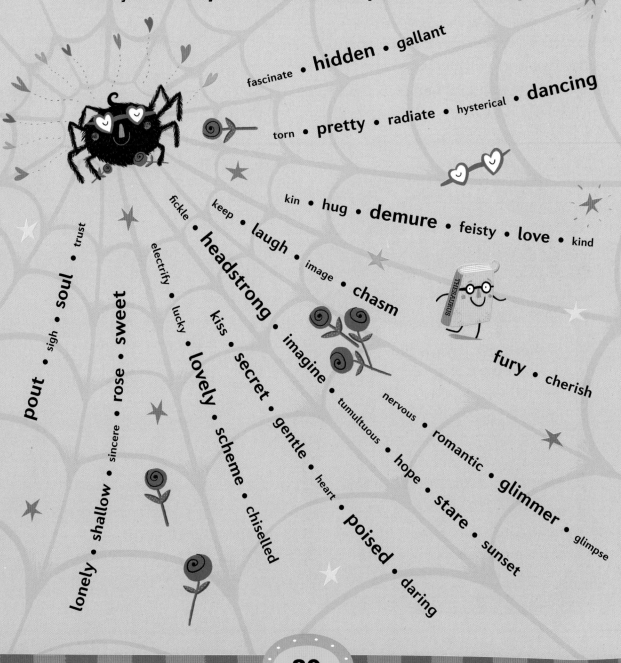

fascinate • **hidden** • **gallant**

torn • **pretty** • radiate • hysterical • **dancing**

kin • **hug** • **demure** • feisty • **love** • kind

fickle • keep • **laugh** • image • **chasm**

electrify • **headstrong** • imagine

trust • sigh • **soul** • **sweet** • **rose**

pout • lucky • kiss • **secret** • **lovely**

lonely • shallow • sincere • scheme • gentle • heart • chiselled

nervous • romantic • **glimmer** • glimpse

tumultuous • hope • stare • sunset

poised • daring

fury • cherish

They say two's company and three's a crowd—but introducing extra characters can add interest and excitement to your story. Maybe you could include a funny best friend for your hero to confide in, or how about a handsome love rival who will challenge him for the heart of your heroine?

Finally, you'll need to decide whether to give your readers a happy ending—or will there be heartbreak on the horizon?

INSPIRATION STATION

Descriptive details can help make a love story feel realistic.

Really attractive people, like Lana and Josh, don't ever go anywhere alone. They always have this sort of entourage that follows them around. — *THE PRINCESS DIARIES* by Meg Cabot

One last kiss, rushed and clumsy so that they banged cheekbones. — *THE AMBER SPYGLASS* by Philip Pullman

Author says . . .

Romance is about conflict as well as kissing! Think of problems and arguments that could keep your couple apart.

What would your characters do for love? Think about the challenges they might have to overcome in the story in order to be together.

Make your readers care about both of your characters.

Your reader should be hoping for a happy ending even if you don't give them one.

RED ALERT!

Adjectives can compare and contrast things.

- For most adjectives, if you are comparing two things, add **-er** to the adjective. This is called the **comparative**.

- For most adjectives, if you are comparing more than two things, add **-est**. This is called the **superlative**.
  Brad was **hot**, Justin was **hotter**, but Theo was the **hottest** boy in school.

Try using comparatives or superlatives to describe any love triangles in your story!

91

How to Write Your Best
HISTORICAL STORY Ever!

When you've got the whole of history to choose from you'll never run out of story ideas. Whether it's writing an adventure about 17th-century pirates swashbuckling across the seven seas or plotting a dramatic tale of soldiers and spies set in the Second World War, the idea you choose can bring the past to life for your readers.

Your story could be inspired by real events from history, such as the Great Fire of London or the Viking invasion of Britain. You could also include actual historical figures like Queen Victoria or Winston Churchill. Try not to mix these up in the same story though!

The Language of History

Which of these words could you use to bring the past to life?

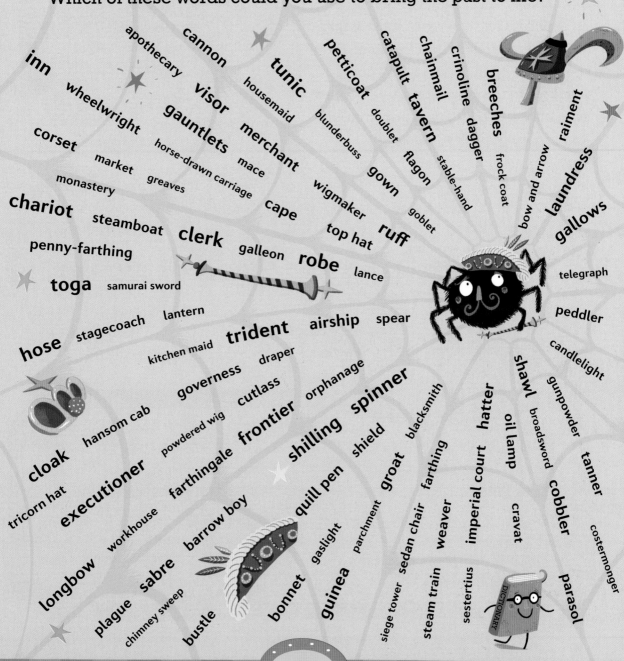

cannon

apothecary

inn

tunic

petticoat

catapult tavern

chainmail

crinoline

breeches

raiment

visor

housemaid

doublet

dagger

stable-hand

frock coat

wheelwright

gauntlets

merchant

mace

blunderbuss

gown

flagon

bow and arrow

laundress

corset

market

horse-drawn carriage

wigmaker

goblet

gallows

monastery

greaves

cape

ruff

chariot

steamboat

clerk

galleon

robe

top hat

lance

telegraph

penny-farthing

toga

samurai sword

peddler

hose

stagecoach

lantern

trident

airship

spear

candlelight

kitchen maid

draper

gunpowder

tanner

governess

cutlass

shawl

broadsword

costermonger

cloak

hansom cab

powdered wig

frontier

orphanage

shilling

spinner

hatter

oil lamp

cobbler

tricorn hat

executioner

farthingale

quill pen

shield

blacksmith

imperial court

cravat

parasol

longbow

workhouse

barrow boy

gaslight

groat

farthing

weaver

plague

sabre

bustle

bonnet

guinea

parchment

sedan chair

steam train

sesterius

chimney sweep

siege tower

Research can help you find out more about what life was really like in the time and place where your story is set. This can stop you from making any silly mistakes such as giving a Victorian explorer a GPS to help them search for lost treasure.

Dropping in details from your research can help your story feel more real, but be careful not to turn your tale into a boring history lesson.

INSPIRATION STATION

Descriptive details can help show the reader when the story takes place.

Warlords and brigands roam the countryside burning and pillaging at will.
— *ARTHUR, HIGH KING OF BRITAIN* by Michael Morpurgo

We were met at the landing place by a file of musketeers and escorted to the fort.
— *PIRATES!* by Celia Rees

It had been raining, and thick mud mingled with the horse-dung in the streets.
— *ORANGES AND MURDER* by Alison Prince

Turn around!

RED ALERT!

In a historical story some characters might speak using formal language.

It is anticipated that all housemaids will attend. Indeed, full attendance is required.

Other characters might speak using **informal language.**
"I didn't see nothing."

95

How to Write Your Best
DIARY STORY Ever!

Have you ever kept a diary or maybe even sneaked a read of somebody else's? A diary writer doesn't just tell you what has happened in their day, but shares their thoughts, feelings, and secrets too.

Anyone can keep a diary, so think about whose story you would like to tell. How about writing the diary of a mythical creature like the Minotaur or the captain's log of the commander of a spaceship on a mission to the stars?

The Language of Diaries

Think about how the words in the web could help you write your diary story.

lies • facts • enemies •

problems • school • comments • disasters

wishes

moments • past • promises

Dear Diary • honest • record

future

memoir • home

social life

day • chronicle • questions • confide • bullies • embarrassing moments

shocks • celebrations

feelings • log

thoughts • plans

truth • days out

emotions

logbook • personal • scrapbook

dreams

journal • date • informal

secrets

gossip

doodles • worries • blog

travel

truth

surprises

advice

fears • hopes

events

trust

A diary story is always written in the first person. Try to create a voice for your diary writer that's one of a kind. How do they look at the world? Through rose-tinted spectacles or gloomy glasses? What words would they use to describe their life?

Remember you're writing a story —not a real diary—so you'll need a beginning, middle, and end. Don't run out of steam in the middle of January!

Diary stories can make the narrator feel very real to the reader.

First of all, let me get something straight: This is a JOURNAL, not a diary. I know what it says on the cover, but when Mom went out to buy this thing I SPECIFICALLY told her to get one that didn't say "diary" on it. Great. All I need is for some jerk to catch me carrying this book around and get the wrong idea. — **THE DIARY OF A WIMPY KID by Jeff Kinney**

No football, no PlayStation, no TV, no nothing. All I'm allowed to do is my homework and tidy my room—the two most boring things in the world, apart from washing the car, which I'm still forced to do for free. — **I'M DOUGAL TRUMP AND IT'S NOT MY FAULT! by Jackie Marchant**

RED ALERT!

Diary stories can use informal punctuation such as **dashes** instead of commas or semicolons. **Capital letters, exclamation marks**, and **question marks** can also be used by the bagful!

You're never going to believe what happened today —I got DETENTION again!!!

Author says . . .

You can make your diary story serious or funny. Write about someone's life today or find inspiration by reading old diaries written hundreds of years ago.

You could write the diary of a real-life person from history such as King Henry VIII or Florence Nightingale.

Or use a diary to describe an everyday person's eyewitness view of an incredible event from history such as the Great Fire of London.

How to Write Your Best ANIMAL STORY Ever!

From wild animal adventures to cuddly pet tales, you can make any creature the star of your story. Choose an animal and think about the skills and talents it has.

Maybe you could make up a story about two squirrels who use their acrobatic skills to fight as tag-team wrestlers. Or change the stereotype to make your character unlike any other animals of this kind. How about a story about a workaholic cat or a donkey who outruns a racehorse. You could even create a new animal such as an elephonkey!

Weird animal facts are another good source of inspiration. Did you know that a baby panda is as small as a mouse when it's born? Or a flamingo can only eat with its head upside down? Think about the stories you could make up from the facts you find out.

The Language of Animals

Use some of the words in the web to describe the animals in your story.

spring
powerful
thick
thorny
nuzzle
woolly
scuttle
nimble
skip
leathery
shaggy
gallop
gleaming
lumber
piebald
iridescent
slink
preen
spotted
crouch
paw
gambol
tough
smooth
stamp
pounce
scaly
glossy
sinewy
silky
leap
spiky
matted
dappled
hop
swoop
hairy
wiry
prickly
glistening
fluffy
coarse
mighty
glide
shiny
dart
circle
hover
stampede
mottled
peck
slimy
perch
slippery
speckled
fly
lumbering
ruffled
muscular
waddle
pad
downy
creep
roam
wiry
bedraggled
majestic
wheel
sleek
agile
soar
bound
furry
slither
striped
drab
trot
flit
skim

Watching animals in real life can help you to make your writing more realistic. Make notes about their behavior —the way they move, how they act —and try to drop these descriptive details into your story.

Use all of the five senses to describe their world. What would a busy city park smell like to a dog? What would a mole hear if someone started digging up their burrow? This can help you to find the voice of your animal character.

INSPIRATION STATION

The right verbs can help to describe an animal's movements and actions.

Varjak slunk towards the wall, willing himself to disappear. — *VARJAK PAW* by S. F. Said

The small rabbit came closer to his companions, lolloping on long hind legs. — *WATERSHIP DOWN* by Richard Adams

Author says . . .

Giving the animals in your story human emotions will help your readers to relate to them. Put yourself in their paws to think about how they might feel in different situations.

RED ALERT!

A **collective noun** refers to a group of animals, such as a **swarm** of bees or a **flock** of sheep. If you're writing a funny animal story you could mix up the collective nouns to describe a flock of bees or a swarm of sheep!

How to Write Your Best SPORTS STORY Ever!

From last-minute equalizers to split-second winners, the best sporting moments can be filled with action, excitement, and emotion—all the ingredients that make a great story. But at the heart of every great story should be characters that your readers can root for.

Think about what your main character wants to achieve. Whether it's a substitute player waiting for his chance to break into the first team or a teenage sprinter going for Olympic gold, giving your main character a goal to reach will help you to develop the plot of your story.

The Language of Sport

Which of these words could you use in your sporting story?

goal

opponents

arena

final whistle

stadium

injury time

extra time

halftime

first half

foul

penalty

possession

sending off

referee

quarter-final

hat trick

kick-off

semi-final

spare

key player

on target

elation

team captain

tactics

strike

supporters

chant

game plan

out of bounds

holler

substitute

man or woman of the match

highlights

score sheet

disappointment

player

heats

squad

amateur

offside

second half

coach

full time

teammate

turning point

qualifying round

trophy

THESAURUS

champion

draw

serve

in play

penalty

commentator

Paralympics

Olympics

professional

Using sporting vocabulary such as "penalty," "out of bounds," and "dribble" can help make your story feel more realistic, but don't get bogged down trying to explain the offside rule!

Most of the action of your story might take place off the field rather than on it. Focus on writing scenes that move the plot forward—an argument with the star hitter on the first pitch or a gangster putting pressure on the manager to play his daughter in the game.

Author says . . .

You can use the sport you choose as the setting to tell different types of stories from laugh-out-loud comedies to action-packed thrillers.

You might even decide to invent your own sport like Quidditch in Harry Potter.

INSPIRATION STATION

Action can be described from the viewpoint of the player or the spectator.

With one minute remaining in the game, Arsenal equalized, unexpectedly and bizarrely, a diving header from a rebound off the goalkeeper's knee. — *FEVER PITCH* by Nick Hornby

I was hopeless. I couldn't tackle. I missed the ball by a mile when I jumped up to head it. — *SKELLIG* by David Almond

RED ALERT!

If you're writing a soccer story, you can use **verbs** such as **bounce, dribble, kick, lob, strike, swerve, header,** and **volley** to describe the action.

How to Write Your Best SCHOOL STORY Ever!

You might not think it when you're looking out of the classroom window on a wet Wednesday afternoon, but you can find inspiration for thousands of fantastic stories in school.

From a class that can't stop laughing to a school run by robot teachers, look around your own school and let your imagination run wild to find ideas for your own story.

You don't need to stay inside school when choosing a setting for your story. How about a school trip to a museum where the dinosaur skeletons come to life or a sports day where the slowest girl in school wins every race by wearing rocket-powered sneakers?

The Language of School

Which of these words could you use in your school story?

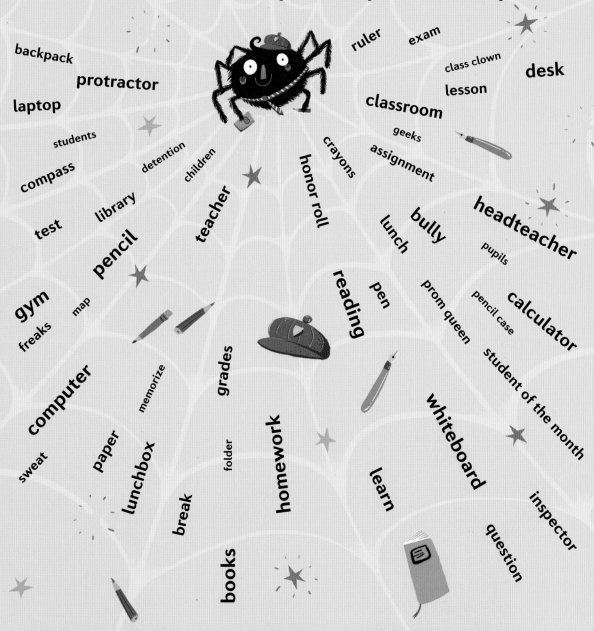

backpack

protractor

laptop

ruler   exam

class clown   desk

lesson

classroom

students

compass   detention   children

crayons   assignment   geeks

test   library   teacher   honor roll   bully   headteacher

pencil   lunch   pupils

gym   map   reading   pen   prom queen   pencil case   calculator

freaks

computer   memorize   grades   student of the month

sweat   paper   lunchbox   folder   homework   whiteboard   inspector

break   learn   question

books

School bullies, best friends, crazy teachers—create a character profile for each of the main characters in your story.

Think about what each character wants—this might be to escape from detention or have the teachers discipline the worst-behaved kids in school. When two characters want opposite things this can create a conflict that brings your story to life.

So what are you waiting for? Finish up your homework and start writing the best school story ever instead!

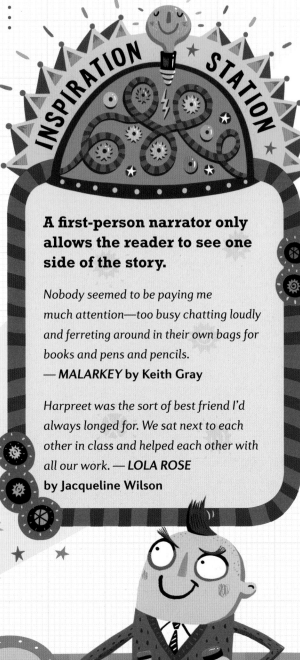

INSPIRATION STATION

A first-person narrator only allows the reader to see one side of the story.

Nobody seemed to be paying me much attention—too busy chatting loudly and ferreting around in their own bags for books and pens and pencils.
— *MALARKEY* by Keith Gray

Harpreet was the sort of best friend I'd always longed for. We sat next to each other in class and helped each other with all our work. — *LOLA ROSE*
by Jacqueline Wilson

Author says . . .

Try keeping a diary and write about what happens in school. You might find inspiration for a fantastic story, but remember to change the characters' names.

You can make school the setting for lots of different types of story.

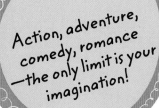

Action, adventure, comedy, romance —the only limit is your imagination!

RED ALERT!

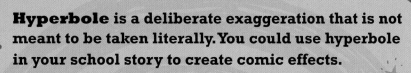

Hyperbole is a deliberate exaggeration that is not meant to be taken literally. You could use hyperbole in your school story to create comic effects.

I've got a pile of homework a mile high.

It was so cold in school today there was a polar bear in the playground.

Victoria Ward had a booger the size of Australia hanging from her nose.

How to Write Your Best
THRILLER STORY Ever!

A thriller is a story where danger lurks around every corner and your main character faces a race against time to make things right. From a search for a kidnapped hamster to a boy on the run from a mysterious foe, your story needs to send your reader on a thrilling roller coaster ride filled with excitement and fear.

Try to create suspense in every scene of your story. You could do this by including details that add to the sense of danger, such as a shadow falling across your hero's back or the sudden ring of a cell phone in a stolen jacket.

The Language of Thrillers

Try to use some of this thrilling vocabulary in your story.

captivity • heist

kidnap • chase • mystery

criminals • problem

ransom • agents • innocent victims

sneak

investigation

prisoners • mission

menace

fear

villain

attack

sabotage • enemy • surveillance

gun • bomb

murder

action • escape • ruthless

danger • shadow • gun

revenge • mistaken identity • police

crime • fight

creep

surveillance • terrorists

assassins

conspiracy

Plot twists can keep your readers guessing about what's going to happen next. Make a list of five unexpected things that could happen in your story. Plant clues about each plot twist to give eagle-eyed readers hints before you hit them with the surprise.

As the clock ticks, keeping up a fast pace will add to the excitement of your story. Will your main character conquer the danger they've faced or will they run out of time?

INSPIRATION STATION

Showing the main character's thoughts and emotions can help build tension.

Every muscle ached to stop, to give up. It was only his brain that kept him going.
— *ON THE EDGE* **by Gillian Cross**

Katie darted one quick glance behind her. She'd never get away from them.
— *RUN, ZAN, RUN* **by Cathy MacPhail**

RED ALERT!

Pronouns are words such as **I, he, she, it, who, this, that**, or **those**. Pronouns are used to replace a noun or noun phrase and help avoid having to repeat words. Think about how you can use pronouns to clearly describe the action in your story.

Zoe and I sneaked into the security complex. She had a pass, but I didn't. The guards were following us and we were unable to shake them off.

Author says . . .

Focus on the action that matters. Start a scene as late as possible and end it as soon as you can. This will keep your thriller moving at a rapid pace.

Cut any scenes that don't keep your story moving.

Try to create a killer ending, but don't bump off your hero if you're planning a sequel!

3

How to Write Your Best SCRIPT Ever!

Whether you want to make a science fiction film or a play like Shakespeare, a superhero comic book, or a TV detective show, you'll need to write a script to bring your ideas to life.

The two most important things you need to include in your script are:

• **dialogue**—what the characters in your story say, and

• **action**—what the characters in your story do or what happens to them.

You have to set out your script in a special way. Don't include lots of description—only write what the audience will see and hear.

KAZOOOOM!

The Language of Scripts

Think about the features you might use in your script. Some will be used in all types of scripts, but other features such as panels, word and thought balloons are only used in comic book scripts.

characters

scenes

description

captions

stage directions

locations

dialogue

sound effects

action

settings

acts

panels

special effects

thought balloon

voiceover

cast

word balloon

Break your story down into scenes to help you write your script. Every time you change to a new time or place, that's the signal to start a new scene.

Remember your script will need a beginning, a middle, and an end. Whether it's an explosive finale to a blockbuster film or a cliff-hanger ending to a TV show, think about how you can keep your audience entertained to the very last line of your script.

INSPIRATION STATION

In a script characters' names are presented in capitals and stage directions placed between parentheses.

"Ghost of the Future," he exclaimed, "I fear you more than any spectre I have seen."
—A CHRISTMAS CAROL by Charles Dickens

SCROOGE: *(shouting) Ghost of the Future, I fear you more than any spectre I have seen.* **—SCRIPT VERSION**

Author says . . .

If you want to write a film or TV show, think about how long this should be. Write the script on a computer, using a 12-point type size.

One 8½ x 11 page equals about one minute of screen time, so if you write a 60-page script this should last an hour.

RED ALERT!

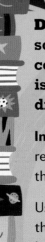

Direct speech is when you write the exact words someone says. In a story it is shown by using inverted commas or quotation marks, but in a script a colon is used after a character's name to introduce their dialogue.

Indirect speech is when a speaker's words are reported by somebody else without using the exact words spoken.

Using **indirect speech** in a script can inform the reader about dialogue which hasn't been shown on the screen, stage, or page.

How to Write Your Best MASH-UP STORY Ever!

From zombies in hats falling in love to dinosaurs flying a spaceship, when you write a mash-up story you can let your imagination run wild.

Take different genres and smash them together to see what story comes out of the explosion. How about a science fiction mystery, an action-adventure comedy, or a spy romance? Think about the typical ingredients of the different genres you're mashing —plots, characters, settings—and pick and mix from these ingredients to make your own story.

The Language of Mash-up

Mix different genres from the web to make your own mash-up.

science fiction

fable

chick-flick

fantasy

scary

superhero

sports

historical

thriller

mystery

crime

animal

chick-lit

adventure

school

myth

diary

gangster

detective

ghost

classic

western

war

horror

romance

comedy

disaster

military

spy

legend

fairy tale

Autobiography

steampunk

Gothic

Mixing up characters from different books, films, and TV shows can be another fun way to think up a plot for a mash-up story. For example, Sherlock Holmes could team up with Little Red Riding Hood to solve *The Mystery of the Grandmother with Extremely Large Teeth*!

Taking characters from one genre and dropping them into a setting taken from another type of story can also create interesting tales. How about a story set in Tolkien High School for Heroes where students have to learn how to slay a dragon or rescue a princess?

Have fun creating your own mash-up story!

Author says . . .

You can mix together different ingredients from books, films, TV, and video games to make an exciting new story.

INSPIRATION STATION

Which of these mash-ups would you like to read?

Jilly had always secretly thought how marvellous it would be to have a dragon as a pet. — *DRAGON RIDE* **by Helen Cresswell**

Signora Strega-Borgia bid the children a tearful farewell and set off to complete her degree in advanced witchcraft. — *PURE DEAD MAGIC* **by Debi Gliori**

"There is no mystery, my dear," said Holmes, smiling. "I see you are in possession of a basket of cakes—the perfect gift for any ailing granny. However, from the marks on your red jacket, I deduce that you have recently had a close encounter with a rather large wolf." — *THE MYSTERY OF THE GRANDMOTHER WITH EXTREMELY LARGE TEETH*

RED ALERT!

A **parody** is a story that copies another story in an exaggerated way in order to make fun of it. Think of any story that you'd like to parody. How might you change the character, setting, and plot to make the reader laugh?

READ ALL ABOUT IT!

Congratulations! If you've reached this page in the book, you must have finished writing your first story. But as soon as a reader finishes reading your story, they're going to want to read more! So what's your next story going to be about?

Every great writer is always on the lookout for inspiration. The great books you read can be terrific places to find ideas. Choose one of these fantastic opening lines to inspire your own story.

When the doorbell rings at three in the morning, it's never good news.
— **STORMBREAKER by Anthony Horowitz**

The island of Gont, a single mountain that lifts its peak a mile above the storm-racked Northeast Sea, is a land famous for wizards.
— **THE WIZARD OF EARTHSEA by Ursula Le Guin**

Kidnapping children is never a good idea; all the same, sometimes it has to be done.
— **THE ISLAND OF THE AUNTS by Eva Ibbotson**

There was a hand in the darkness, and it held a knife.
— **THE GRAVEYARD BOOK by Neil Gaiman**

It's a funny thing about mothers and fathers. Even when their own child is the most disgusting little blister you could ever imagine, they still think that he or she is wonderful.
— **MATILDA by Roald Dahl**

Johnny never knew for certain why he started seeing the dead. — **JOHNNY AND THE DEAD by Terry Pratchett**

My family spend every holiday in a caravan by the sea. All of us get stuffed into a bedroom the size of a car boot. We sleep with the window open. If you have brothers, then you know why. — **THE LEGEND OF CAPTAIN CROW'S FEET** by Eoin Colfer

In a hole in the ground there lived a hobbit. — **THE HOBBIT** by J.R.R. Tolkien

I write this sitting in the kitchen sink. — **I CAPTURE THE CASTLE** by Dodie Smith

There is no lake at Green Camp Lake. — **HOLES** by Louis Sachar

How five crows managed to lift a twenty-pound baby boy into the air was beyond Prue, but that was certainly the least of her worries. — **WILDWOOD** by Colin Meloy

Whatever it was, it could only have been dead for a couple of hours. — **THE FEARFUL** by Keith Gray

Sometimes there's no warning. — **OATH BREAKER** by Michelle Paver

There was no doubt about it: there was a fox behind the climbing frame. And it was watching. — **UN LUN DUN** by China Mieville

The tapping on the window woke him. — **A DOG SO SMALL** by Philippa Pearce

It was dusk, winter-dusk. — **THE WOLVES OF WILLOUGHBY CHASE** by Joan Aiken

Author says . . .

If you're running low on inspiration, reading can give you fuel for your fiction. Keep your eyes peeled —ANYTHING could give you the spark for a new story.

Whatever ideas you choose, keep writing brilliant stories that will inspire your readers too!

INDEX

A

action 21, 24, 29, 32, 34–37, 60, 63, 82, 84, 86, 102, 104, 106, 107, 115, 116

adjective 17, 44, 63, 78, 91

adventure story 60–63, 92, 100

adverb 44, 63

animal story 100–103

antonym 41

apostrophe 67

archaic words and spellings 79

B

beginning 22, 30–33, 52, 57, 60, 84, 98, 115, 118

C

character 10, 12, 14–17, 20, 21, 22, 24, 26–28, 32, 38, 42, 44–45, 46, 48, 49, 50, 52, 54, 57, 60, 62, 66, 69, 70, 72, 74–75, 76–77, 82, 86, 88, 90, 95, 100, 102, 104, 110, 112, 114, 116, 118–119, 120, 122

clause 25, 87

cliché 36, 53, 59, 71, 86

cliff-hanger 52–53, 86, 118

collective noun 103

comedy 30, 72–75, 90, 103, 106, 111, 120

comic book 116–119

comic story 30, 72–75, 90, 103, 106, 120

conflict 90, 110

conjunction 25, 87

crime story 64–67, 112

D

description 16, 21, 26, 28, 32, 34, 36, 38–41, 49, 57, 60, 63, 74, 82, 90, 94, 102, 106, 116

dialogue 32, 42–45, 57, 116, 119

diary 111

diary story 96–99, 111

E

ellipsis 53

emotion 26, 28, 37, 51, 86, 96, 103, 104, 114

ending 12, 14, 22, 50–53, 66, 86, 90, 118

event 22, 24, 25, 32, 33, 34–37, 50, 52, 54, 60, 69, 70, 92

F

fantasy 18, 20, 76–79

feelings 26, 28, 37, 51, 86, 96, 103, 104, 114

first-person narrator 26–28, 74, 96–99, 110

formal language 95

funny story 30, 72–75, 90, 103, 106, 120

futuristic story 80–83

G

genre 11, 120, 123

H

hero, heroine 14, 16, 36, 38, 40, 42, 48, 50, 52, 56, 60, 62, 63, 70, 75, 76, 84, 86, 90, 112

historical story 20, 92–95

history 20, 92–95

humour 72–75, 90, 99, 103, 106, 111

hyperbole 111

hyphen 75

I

ideas 10, 12, 13, 20, 22, 24–25, 48, 54, 63, 72, 76, 79, 80, 92, 108, 116

informal language 95

inspiration 10, 12, 63, 72, 82, 92, 99, 100, 108, 111

inverted commas or speech marks 45, 119

L

landscape 19

love story 26, 88–91, 120

M

map 18, 20, 78

mash-up story 54, 120–123

metaphor 40–41, 66

mood 20, 51

mystery story 30, 44, 50, 54, 64–67, 120, 122

N

name 16, 45, 84, 111, 118–119

noun 13, 17, 62, 103, 115

O

onomatopoeia 49

opening 22, 30–33, 52, 57, 60, 84, 98, 115, 118

P

pace 57, 70, 98, 114, 115

parody 123

paragraph 33, 45

place 10, 12, 18–21, 32, 38, 46, 54, 57, 62–63, 69, 77, 78, 82, 94, 108, 118, 120

play 116–119

plot 12, 14, 16, 22–25, 32, 37, 44, 50, 56, 57, 72, 76, 80, 82, 86, 87, 92, 104, 106, 114, 120, 122

preposition 21

pronoun 115

punctuation 45, 99

R

reaction 14, 36

red herring 67

research 18, 20, 99, 100

review 45, 56–59

revision 57, 58

S

scary story 68–71

scene 20, 34, 36–37, 40, 46, 56–57, 70, 72, 106, 112, 115, 118

school story 108–111

science fiction 18, 20, 80–83, 116, 120

script 116–119

sensation 18, 39

senses 36, 38, 70, 102

sentence 25, 29, 53, 87

setting 10, 12, 18–21, 32, 38, 46, 54, 57, 62–63, 69, 77, 78, 82, 94, 106, 108, 118, 120, 122

sight 13, 18, 38, 40, 57, 70

simile 40–41, 66, 74

smell 13, 18, 39, 70, 102

sound 13, 18, 36, 39, 49, 70, 102

speech 42–45, 57, 116, 119

spelling 59

sports story 104–107

spy story 18, 84–87, 92, 120

stage direction 118

suspense 52, 66, 70, 87, 112

synonym 41

T

taste 13, 39, 70

telling the story 26–29, 98–99, 110

tense (verb) 29, 35

tension 70, 86, 112, 114

third-person narrator 28

thriller 18, 106, 112–115

title 54–55

tone 27, 30, 42

touch 13, 70

type of story 11, 30, 54–55, 106, 120–122

V

verb 29, 35, 37, 43, 62, 87, 102, 107

villain 6, 14, 16, 42, 62, 66, 86

vocabulary 46–49, 73, 79, 83, 85, 106, 113

voice 26–27, 32, 42, 57, 98, 102

W

weather 20